3/03

window treatment

Decorating Ideas

Better Homes and Gardens Books
Des Moines, Iowa

Better Homes and Gardens® Books
An imprint of Meredith® Books

Window Treatment Decorating Ideas
Editors: Linda Hallam, Brian Kramer
Contributing Editor: Amber Barz
Design: The Design Office of Jerry J. Rank
Copy Chief: Terri Fredrickson
Copy and Production Editor: Victoria Forlini
Editorial Operations Manager: Karen Schirm
Managers, Book Production: Pam Kvitne, Marjorie J. Schenkelberg
Contributing Copy Editor: Jane Woychick
Contributing Proofreaders: Kathi DiNicola, Vivian Mason
Indexer: Sharon Duffy
Electronic Production Coordinator: Paula Forest
Editorial and Design Assistants: Kaye Chabot, Mary Lee Gavin, Karen McFadden

Meredith® Books
Publisher and Editor in Chief: James D. Blume
Design Director: Matt Strelecki
Managing Editor: Gregory H. Kayko
Executive Editor, Home Decorating and Design: Denise L. Caringer

Director, Operations: George A. Susral
Director, Production: Douglas M. Johnston

Vice President and General Manager: Douglas J. Guendel

Better Homes and Gardens® Magazine
Editor in Chief: Karol DeWulf Nickell

Meredith Publishing Group
President, Publishing Group: Stephen M. Lacy
Vice President-Publishing Director: Bob Mate

Meredith Corporation
Chairman and Chief Executive Officer: William T. Kerr

Chairman of the Executive Committee: E. T. Meredith III

All of us at Better Homes and Gardens® Books are dedicated to providing you with information and ideas to enhance your home. We welcome your comments and suggestions. Write to us at: Better Homes and Gardens Books, Home Decorating and Design Editorial Department, 1716 Locust St., Des Moines, IA 50309-3023.

If you would like to purchase any of our home decorating and design, cooking, crafts, gardening, or home improvement books, check wherever quality books are sold. Or visit us at: bhgbooks.com

contents

4 **gettingstarted** Prepare to get the most from your windows.

26 **hometour** Plan treatments that flow beautifully from one room to the next.

50 **roomtour** Dress windows to match the form and function of each room in your home.

70 **draperies&curtains** Adorn your windows with flowing fabrics.

90 **shades,shutters&blinds** Explore the latest innovations.

108 **toptreatments** Add boundless style with exciting toppings.

126 **combinations** Have it all, beautifully and practically.

144 **help&how-to** Learn about fabric selection, window styles, and treatment installation.

gettingstarted

Nothing adds more design flair to a room than the right window treatment. Window treatments can **highlight or enhance your home's architectural style, warm or cool a room, and even camouflage an imperfection or two.** For totally successful treatments, pretty must work hand in hand with practical.

Consider your needs for privacy and light control. Gauzy swags may complement your white-wicker-furnished breakfast room, but if the windows are drafty, you may need to install insulating shades beneath the swags. **If you want your windows to admit as much light as possible,** opt for top treatments alone, or combine top treatments with sheer panels that softly diffuse light.

Take airflow and traffic patterns into consideration too. Puddles of silk flowing from a dining room window add sumptuous atmosphere, but puddles are less than practical if the fabric inhibits access to a patio door. The top treatment and side panels on the French door *above* were carefully measured to stay clear of the door's path of operation.

An average home has between 20 and 30 windows. **To find enough inspiration to adorn them all, see Home Tour, beginning on page 26, and Room Tour, beginning on page 50.** While taking an armchair tour of whole houses and individual room settings, **keep in mind the mood of the existing furnishings and fabrics in each of your rooms.** For the most pleasing look, choose window treatment fabrics and styles that match the degree of formality in each room.

As this chapter demonstrates, you can **highlight the most attractive windows in**

your home by assigning them the most striking window treatments. Let strictly functional windows fade into the backdrop with less-conspicuous window fare. **Use complementary treatments in rooms that open to one another or that share the same style of furnishings.** For example, use the same fabrics in your kitchen and adjoining breakfast room; choose complementary window treatments for your formal dining area and adjacent living room.

For a fail-safe whole-house window treatment plan, mix and match only two or three classic styles throughout your entire home, such as drapery panels and wooden blinds combined with fabric valances that match your upholstered furnishings. **If your window styles and sizes vary within a room, use the same fabric but in different fabrications,** such as Roman shades mixed with tab-top panels in the same cotton print. For a clear picture of how to enhance every room in your home with fabulous window decorating ideas, turn the page.

FindingInspiration

Begin your search for the right window treatment by finding design inspiration from the things you cherish most.

LOOK AROUND. INSPIRATION FOR DECORATING YOUR WINDOWS MAY COME FROM SOMETHING YOU ALREADY OWN. A cherished vase, a striking painting, or a favorite upholstery fabric can reveal your color palette preferences, as well as your taste for formal or casual styles.

Take a tour through your clothing closet. The styles and colors you wear may reveal the colors you're most comfortable living in. Your home decor surrounds you every day, so what you choose for window treatments should be as appealing to you as what you wear.

Do you like tailored clothing and vintage furnishings? Classic swags and draperies complement a crisp, traditional scheme. Are blue jeans and flannel shirts more your style? Perky curtains and gathered valances enhance casual and country looks. Like a little romance? Balloon shades and billowing top treatments create a romantic backdrop for feminine fabrics and furnishings. Is sleek and understated your preference? Choose blinds, shutters, or shades and dispense with the unnecessary flair. For examples of window treatments that fit an array of decorating styles, see page 26.

■ Inspired by French doors, drapery panels on hinged rods make opening and closing the windows easy. Flowing white-striped sheers veil the windows when the curtains are closed. When open, the treatment creates an illusion of movement and access to the outdoors.

Whatever your style preference, don't let your window treatment's form impede its function. If light control is an issue, choose treatments that are easy to adjust. If you plan to open and close your windows during temperate months, choose treatments that you can pull out of the way while the window is open.

■ Wooden shutters *above* add cottage charm to this cozy breakfast area and enable diners to control the light to match the time of day. The white-painted louvered shutters complement the divided-light windows and add more textural interest to the room.

■ Floor-to-ceiling bay windows are an obvious focal point, but knowing how to trim them can be a less-than-obvious affair. In this romantic sunroom *left,* a checked-chintz-covered rod extends across the top of all the windows, making the six separate panes appear as one. Two sets of gathered swags in two different fabrics are cinched at alternate points to top off the windows. Four full-length, ivy-leaf fabric panels can be closed to curb sunlight.

■DESIGN TIP Think about how your windows open and close before narrowing your choice of window treatments. Double-hung windows that slide open and closed can be adorned with almost any treatment. However, some French doors and casement windows open in and require treatments that don't get in the way of their path of operation. Does your window have a crank handle? If so, the handle may interfere with slats or louvers, particularly if you want your treatments mounted inside the window casements.

■ The tieback panel *below* is installed so that it doesn't interfere with the French door. Sheer linen windowpane-check privacy panels draw in front of the door when more privacy is desired. Striped draperies have been stitched from three panels of fabric to create fullness.

SOLUTIONS FOR SUN & PRIVACY. Shutters, shades, and blinds come in different styles, sizes, and materials, yet they all fill the same practical role. They are excellent choices for both light control and privacy and they can be used as starting points for almost any window treatment. If you prefer a minimalist look, choose fabric blinds or shades that can be rolled or pulled up and out of sight. Or choose cellular pleated shades that shield the view from the bottom of the window to whatever height you desire.

■ Draperies and balloon shades tend to be an all-or-nothing affair; they are either open or closed. Layer these shades on top of sheer panels or blinds.

■ Simple miniblinds are ideal for children's rooms, but check that cords are properly installed and well out of reach of young children. Avoid imported vinyl blinds; some contain lead.

■ If your home is relatively new, heat loss and gain through your windows may not be an issue because many of today's windows are energy efficient. Drafty, older windows, however, may be a significant source of heat loss during the winter and heat gain during the summer. To remedy this, consider choosing thermally insulated fabrics, shades, or blinds. Treatments that offer thermal insulation are usually advertised as such. Textiles such as wool, velvet, brocade, damask, and silk also minimize radiant heat loss or gain.

■ Hot sun requires durable fabrics. The sheer underdrapery *above* is polyester—necessary to endure the strong sunlight in this south-facing gentleman's bedroom. A loose-weave cotton stripe was used for the tieback panels; wooden bead fringe trims the panel's edge without fuss. Crown molding tops off the upholstered cornice.

■ Swing-arm rods installed at the top and bottom of a sidelight panel *right,* and on a window panel *far right,* support privacy curtains. Installing a swing rod at the top and the bottom prevents the fabric from flapping when the door is opened or closed.

Enhance What You Have

Assess the windows you want to decorate. Do they enhance the architectural style of your home?

ARE THE CASINGS ATTRACTIVE ENOUGH TO HIGHLIGHT OR ARE THEY ODDLY SHAPED LIABILITIES THAT NEED CAMOUFLAGING? HOW ARE THE VIEWS? ARE YOU LOOKING ONTO GARDENS OR YOUR NEIGHBORS' SIDEWALLS?

If your windows are finished with decorative molding that you want to emphasize, make the most of it. Mount your shades inside the window casement and adorn only the window top with a loosely hung swag or valance.

If the view is terrific, draw attention to it and visually increase the size of the window by mounting top treatments higher on the wall than the window itself and mounting side panels so that they clear the window's glazing when open.

Camouflage unattractive views with sheers—the more opaque the better—or with blinds, shutters, or shades. Carefully position blind and shutter slats or louvers to maximize light and obscure the view.

■ In spaces designed to capture as much light as possible, consider opting for simple top treatments on floor-to-ceiling windows. In the relaxed sitting room, 1-inch piping trims the edges of the large fabric triangles that make up the valance. Metal "tassels" accent the lower points, adding a touch of humor to the unusual treatment.

Show off architectural treasures, such as octagonal or circular windows: Leave them untreated or mount custom-made shutters or blinds within the window casings.

Add importance to a small group of windows by dressing them with a single treatment that visually unifies them. Make two adjacent windows appear like one large one by giving each a single drapery pulled back to the far side of either window. To make windows of different sizes and shapes within the same room look more cohesive, dress them with similar treatments made from the same fabrics. If one window is taller, hang all drapery rods or valances at the same height to make the windows appear identical.

■ A passion for Victorian-era furnishings is highlighted by the Kingston-shape valances in a baby's room *above*. Cascading swags join together with flowing fabric tabs that hang from an old-fashioned iron rod.

■ Open drapery panels make the narrow window *opposite* look twice as wide as its actual dimensions. The panels' stacks start at the window's edge, creating the illusion that the window extends to where the treatment ends. Overlaid "necklace" swags in a complementary plaid dress up the panels and tone down their riotous colors. Throw pillows draw the color to the settee that fills the space below the window.

■ Even windowless rooms can benefit from window treatments. The lush vista seen from the powder room alcove *right* is actually an oil painting. The "concha"— a crown-molding-like detail that's common in Spanish architecture—is also faux detailing painted above the window frame. The drapery panels, hung in trumpet pleats from hand-forged iron pegs, bring a sense of reality to the make-believe space.

■ Art glass draws attention to the charming view beyond the sunporch *below*. To keep the focus on the view and the art glass, fabric treatments are kept to a minimum. Linen napkins, sewn from an array of complementary fabrics, drape over simple tension rods inside the tops of the window frames.

■ Not all windows have views that need showcasing. The self-lined silk panel *below* keeps a less-than-attractive view under wraps. Black tassels, trimmed in gold and staggered in length, create visual rhythm and interest. Hand-applied gold leaf on the custom-made cornice adds rich color and keeps the focus on the room rather than the outside.

■ Occupying a slight alcove in the wall, the tall eyebrow window *above* fits flush against its sidewalls, leaving no room for draperies to stack off to the sides. To solve the problem, a custom-made rod that duplicates the shape of the window top was designed. Soldered-on iron rings hold the panels in place. Made from a cotton-rayon blend, the sheer aqua panels are cinched low at the sides with tiebacks. Painting the surrounding woodwork white draws additional attention to the window.

Set The Right Tone

Let the gathering spaces in your home—typically the living area, the dining area, the kitchen, and the family room—reflect your personal decorating style.

FOR AN EASYGOING CASUAL LOOK, EXPLORE THE POSSIBILITIES OF ROMAN SHADES, CAFE CURTAINS, PLEATED SHADES, AND WOODEN SHUTTERS. CASUAL SCHEMES WELCOME INTENSE BURSTS OF COLOR, DRAMATIC PATTERNS, AND FUNKY HARDWARE.

Loosely hung swags add a soft, casual feel to window tops. Simple sheers, gathered denim panels, and tab-top canvas draperies also fit within a casual design theme. Polished cottons such as chintz have a more relaxed look if you wash them first to reduce the sheen. Balloon shades and complicated symmetrical treatments may be too fussy for casual design.

If a formal statement is what you are after, give your windows the full treatment. Formal looks include swagged valances with trims and fringes, jabots, lined side panels, and tasseled tiebacks.

■ Symmetrical designs are common in formal rooms, as shown in this flowing swag-and-jabot and side-panel treatment. Highly tailored valances alone also have a formal look. Requiring a minimum of fabric, they can help keep your budget in check.

Although the most casual fabrics can be shaped into formal drapery, using formal fabric communicates the right attitude from the start. Fabrics with a sheen, such as silks, damasks, and taffetas, along with their synthetic look-alikes, are clearly formal. Heavy velvets and fine tapestries also add a formal edge.

If scene-stealing fabrics don't mix well with the existing materials in your room, consider using elegant braids or beading to dress up plain linen draperies. A formal setting doesn't always mean traditional styling; in the window treatment *opposite top*, lined tieback panels give the room a more contemporary twist.

■ Spice up a room by working in additional patterns within window treatments. The soft green-striped fabric of the Roman shades in the casually dressed family room *above* is a different shade of green and pattern from the plaid sofa fabric, both of which add visual interest. Green molding trim draws the eye to the walls, windows, and the view beyond.

■ To create a crisp but unobtrusive backdrop for more formal furnishings, the botanical-print silk panels *above* are lined in a solid-color fabric that blends with the color of the walls. The fitted panels fold back to reveal attractive yet understated taupe silk.

■ Damask draperies puddle at the sides of the windows and French doors in the living area *left*. The garden doors are rarely used, so fabric flowing onto the floor is not a problem in this setting. The enlarged zigzag edges and casual gathers in the top valance prevent the treatment from looking overly formal. The fabric's tight weave and thickness help keep the room warm during the winter. Cotton undersheers control the light.

■ When window treatment colors are bold, a simple design is often best. The valances in the vibrant dining area *above* are made from the border of a French tablecloth like the one covering the round table. A rod pocket sewn onto the back of the rectangle covers a simple tension rod; the ends of the rectangle drape and fold naturally into points. The tablecloth's gold-tone leaves inspired the color for the room's walls.

■ Old-world, industrial, and tropical influences combine for an amazingly seamless effect in a guest bedroom *right*. Vintage Irish tablecloths purchased from flea markets trim the posts of an iron bed; complementary linens serve as top treatments on the windows. Lace panels offer privacy.

■ A voluminous double-swag treatment disguises the various window sizes in the formal office *above*. Two tall, narrow side windows looked disproportionate next to the short arched center window. To make all three appear the same height, the plaid cotton swags are elevated to crown molding height. The smaller side window receives a "half treatment" of similar design. Golden silk lining adds fullness to each of the swags. Rope cording, tassels, and fringe step up the formalities, making the treatments perfect mates for the coffered, wallpapered ceiling.

hometour

Casual Gem

Savor casual living and timeless style with an array of light and airy window treatments.

FOR A SOFT, CASUAL ATMOSPHERE THAT RELAXES AND CALMS AS YOU MOVE FROM ROOM TO ROOM, CHOOSE SIMPLE WINDOW TREATMENTS THAT KEEP THE FOCUS on architectural aspects of your home, on your furnishings, or on the view outside. A simple, pared-down look is experiencing renewed popularity, and this trend goes hand in hand with casual styling.

For a no-fuss, no-muss feel throughout your home, seek out classic treatment styles—panels, blinds, shutters, and sheers—in rich but non-trendy colors and fabrics. Remember, casual style is all about *you* and how you *really* live each day; the look you choose for your window treatments should be both practical and appealing.

Sheer swags take on a subtle and casual appearance, welcoming in the light and the view. The simplicity of this timeless design makes it an excellent choice for windows where little covering is needed.

Vibrant-color window treatments work well in casual settings, particularly in rooms where upholstery fabrics are solid and subdued in color. The swooping curves of the dining room's yellow, red, and blue cotton print valance *above* mimic the curves of the built-in corner hutches. The valance colors complement the blue denim slipcovers. Drapery panels made from the same fabric as the valance control afternoon light.

■ Cherry red shirred cotton valances *left* and *above* tie together the window treatments in a family room, breakfast room, and kitchen. Gathered panels of creamy white cotton are trimmed in red to add a cheerful punch to the decor in the breakfast room and family room.

■ In the kitchen *left,* the red fabric is left off the panels to make them easier to clean, but the treatments still fit into the overall relaxed scheme.

Wooden plantation shutters let the right amount of light into the west-facing sunroom *above*. Because the upholstered furnishings and kilim rug have lots of color and pattern, no top treatments are added to the shutters.

■**DESIGN TIP** To let in the maximum amount of light with plantation shutters, use the largest panels possible in combination with the widest louvers. However, avoid selecting panels taller than 48 inches because they can be somewhat bulky and difficult to install. Windows wider than 96 inches require extra framing to support the shutters. Check that each shutter has the same number of louvers per panel so that all the windows in the room look unified.

■ For casual simplicity in the master bedroom, translucent, decorative glass panels add sparkle to the clerestory and transom windows *above*. French doors are adorned with sheer fabric horizontal blinds to control the light and provide privacy.

■ Where water and windows meet, simple treatments are smart solutions. A casually knotted swag adds color to the windows above the master bathroom's tub *left*. Aluminum blinds provide privacy and complement the horizontal stripes of the fabric.

TraditionalTreasure

Enhance your traditional setting with full-length symmetrical treatments. Mix classic draperies with light-filtering undersheers or blinds.

THE MAGIC OF TRADITIONAL STYLING LIES IN ITS EVERLASTING DESIGN APPEAL. In formal rooms, choose full, flowing window treatments that complement the fabrics of the furnishings. Use pattern or color to transform a window into a focal point. Elaborate layers of draperies with top treatments are always attention grabbers. Embellishments like tassels and rosettes also catch the eye.

The windows in adjoining rooms don't have to match, but they should coordinate, particularly if you can see both treatments at the same time.

■ Luxurious gold and white striped douppioni silk adorns the living and dining room windows in this historic home. The living room features a combination of bay windows and French doors, so plantation shutters are a better choice than more typical undersheers because they allow for easier access to a deck beyond.

■ Look for color scheme clues in architectural and historical color palettes that correspond to the period of a traditional home. For example, the amber stained glass in the home's stairwell *above* inspired the fabric selection in the living and dining areas.

■ Indulge in traditional luxury with layered waves of beautiful fabric. The dining room's formal window treatment *left* includes a sheer white silk casement curtain, silk draperies tied back with matching silk rope, and a swag-and-jabot fabric valance. The gold-tone fabric used on the dining chairs echoes the color scheme. For a final flourish, gilded drapery tiebacks support the ends of the swags.

■ In kitchens, choose treatments that you can pull up and out of the way when food preparation is in full swing. Inside-mount translucent Roman shades filter light in the kitchen *right*.

■ Rooms full of busy fabrics and accessories call for unassuming window treatments. In the study *below*, exotic animal prints and colorful book jackets contrast with the simple design of narrow-louver wooden shutters that are perfect for controlling the light.

EclecticRetreat

Mix favorite standbys with trendy treatments to create window designs that fit your family's needs.

YOU PUT YOURSELF AND YOUR GUESTS AT EASE WHEN YOU TAILOR YOUR HOME DECOR AND YOUR WINDOW TREATMENT SELECTIONS TO THE WAY YOU REALLY LIVE. For starters, window treatments don't have to be fabric. Top a kitchen window with a display shelf or trim a breakfast room window with a collection of hanging plates.

In the family room *right*, open shelves surround the divided-light windows. Mix and match your window treatments so that they are functional as well as pleasing in form. Instead of using traditional window treatments, frame windows with open shelves that can act as an ever-evolving gallery for collections, art, or photos.

■ In the family room, the windows are high enough that they don't require coverings, and the wash of light they provide highlights the display niches.

■ Create a contemporary feel in a sleekly furnished room with handkerchief valances. Red and black heavy brushed cotton triangular valances draped over a decorative black rod *left* combine simplicity with high style. Full-length draperies control light and provide privacy as necessary.

■ Put a unique aspect of a room center stage with minimalist treatments. A simple pleated shade dresses the window in the retro-look kitchen *below* without distracting from the room's focal point black and white tile backsplash.

Cottage Charm

Relax in the comfort of easy, breezy cottage styling by choosing treatments that calm and refresh.

THE APPEAL OF COTTAGE STYLING LIES IN ITS SIMPLICITY. This romantic style reflects simple human needs and the values associated with country life—time for reflection, harmony with nature, and the company of good friends and family. To apply this easy-living scheme to your windows, choose treatments that are understated and nostalgic. Old-fashioned plaids and subtle stripes are excellent fabric choices.

White-painted plantation shutters or white wooden or vinyl blinds are a sure-fit foundation for this style. Top these sun-sheltering under-treatments with simple valances that comple-ment the traditionally pastel, time-softened cot-tage color scheme. If privacy and sun control aren't a concern, forgo the blinds and choose sim-ple top treatments alone.

■ A simple mix of treatments yields visual variety and a satisfying, pulled-together continuity. Matchstick blinds *right* work as top treatments when rolled up and bound with fabric ties that can be changed to complement new slipcovers or highlight the season. White miniblinds provide sun control. At the far end of the room, stained-glass overlays add year-round floral color to the entryway.

■ Carefully selected bits of vibrant color please the eye and the pocketbook with modest yardage. A scalloped-edge roller shade on the Dutch door *left* adds design impact.

■ Shirred and ruffled valances edged with a yellow French country print *below* brighten the room without breaking the budget. The cheerful fabric pops up in the chandelier shades as well as the tablecloth trim.

■DESIGN TIP If your budget requires you to choose between expensive materials and expensive labor, put your money into the labor. A skilled craftsperson—drapery maker, upholsterer, or carpenter—can make even discount store material look like a million bucks. Use expensive fabrics sparingly on top treatments and trims.

■ The right window treatment can keep cottage style from becoming overly cute. Minimal treatments are the best answer in the pattern-rich master bedroom *above* and *right*. The linen-look ready-made Roman shades are standard department store fare, but for a custom touch, the shades are tied up with blue and white checked dish towels. White wooden blinds are an ideal backdrop, offering privacy when required yet never distracting from the lush backyard view.

roomtour

living&diningrooms

Your decorating preferences and the architectural style of your home point to the perfect window treatments for living and dining areas.

THESE HARDWORKING ROOMS ARE THE PLACE TO PUT MOST OF YOUR DECORATING CREATIVITY TO WORK. A full formal treatment may include a casement curtain, which is installed inside a window's trim area; overdraperies that cover the window's trim and a portion of the adjoining wall; and a top treatment such as swags and jabots or a fabric valance. Less formal treatments may edit the look to little more than a simple scarf valance and attractive window jewelry. Either way, don't overfill the room with fabrics; "less is more" is the design mantra of the day.

■ In the family room *right*, minimal window treatments keep the focus on the furnishings. Red ribbon trim subtly connects the sheer natural linen with accessories and fabrics in the room.

■ When you find a pattern that suits you, repeat and vary it among the elements of a room. The living room *left* combines four different scales of stripes on the walls, furnishings, and tieback draperies. Jute fringe and tiebacks add designer detail to the panels. Sheer windowpane-check undercurtains provide a touch of privacy throughout the day, eliminating the need to untie the overdraperies.

■ Choose valances to inject instant, inexpensive bursts of color into a room. Triangular pennants in vibrant red and yellow billow across the windows in a brightly colored family room, *below left*. Known as a tear-drop valance because of its shape, the treatment's pointed sections are actually separate pieces of fabric that attach to the window frame via cup hooks. Bright red napkin rings cover the hooks and boost the colorful effect.

■ The bold English plaid that generously frames the windows in fringed swags and puddled drapery panels *above* matches the scale of the weighty stone fireplace. The country casual print keeps the room from looking too formal. Briefly repeating the window treatment fabric in toss pillows and a throw ties the window treatments to the furnishings without producing an overly coordinated look.

■ Choosing the right fabric can make all the difference in fashioning great treatments. Stationary valances mounted inside the window frames combine with cafe-style roller shades

opposite top to complement the circa 1930s retro design of the sitting area.

■ Fabric perfects the sophisticated look in the living room *right below*. On the bay window, silk brocade panels are lined in white (for a uniform look from the outside) and trimmed in a contrasting fabric to highlight the warm colors of the camelback chairs. Gathered swags embellish the panels. On the adjacent French doors, a full-length, fully lined swag flows from floor to ceiling, across the transom top, and back to the floor again.

DESIGN TIP Small-scale, low-contrast geometric patterns, such as tone-on-tone checks and ticking stripes, are easy to mix and match. Add fabric focal points with larger scale florals, geometrics, or ethnic prints. In small rooms, use large-scale prints sparingly; too much of a big, busy print can overpower a room. If you are using a small-scale print on window treatments in a large room, pick a vibrantly colored pattern.

■ A dining room *right* displays the tropical influence of botanicals and shades of green. To avoid overwhelming the room, understated tab-top drapery panels add a burst of visual punch in the striped trim.

■ Tall windows in high-ceilinged rooms are perfect candidates for classic drapery and valance treatments. The burgundy and white color scheme accented with black adds dramatic color to a narrow dining space, *opposite far right.* Toile panels adorn the 8-foot-high window. Box pleats incorporated into the valance draw the eye up to the full height of the 14-foot ceiling.

■ Accessories can pull together the furnishings and decor of a room. Shimmering braided rope and matching tassels embellish the pleated sewn-back drapery panels *above.* These sparkly touches complement the golden tones found in the zigzag ivy wallpaper, the painted dining chairs, and the woven rug.

■ Swag and jabot valances hang from hooks that follow the curves of the arch-top dining room windows *right,* highlighting the softly rounded window frames. For an added dash of formality, tieback silk brocade panels undergird the swags and jabots.

■ Blend valance fabric with the background wallpaper to make a subtle transition from window treatment to wall. Scalloped floral valances over the bay window in the breakfast area *left* almost appear to be part of the architecture of the room. Striped linen Roman shades add a touch of contrast.

kitchens

For these casual gathering rooms, choose easy-care treatments that make way for sunlight.

TODAY'S KITCHENS INVITE FRIENDS AND FAMILY TO GATHER AND COOK TOGETHER. Choose colorful fabrics that can either be washed or dry-cleaned. When sun control or privacy is a concern, add shades, shutters, or blinds that can be wiped clean with a damp cloth.

■ Crown molding, extended from the custom-made cabinetry, serves as a cornice board over the bay window in an English country kitchen *above right*. Gathered valances made of two-tone, toile-inspired designer fabric hang on curtain rods installed on the wall behind the molding.

■ A white cutwork table topper thrown over a rod at an angle and flanked by two crisp checkered counterpoints makes an elegant yet economical window treatment in a country kitchen *right* and *opposite*. Tassel fringe gives the simple statement a fillip of finery. Consider using vintage hankerchiefs or linen napkins to create a similar treatment in your kitchen or breakfast room.

DESIGN TIP If you like to clear the air of cooking odors, choose a window covering that doesn't impede airflow. Before choosing treatments, consider the way your windows open and close: Double-hung windows are the easiest windows to dress. French doors and casement windows that swing into a room require treatment designs that do not interfere with their operation.

■ Classic French country print fabrics add a festive air to the windows in this kitchen *above*. Because imported fabrics can be costly, select a treatment that highlights the pattern yet requires only a few yards of fabric. Lined with a complementary stripe fabric of a similar weight, the simple floral chintz valance dangles from decorative hoops that have been threaded over red-painted, rope-molded curtain rods.

■ The griffin-print fabric used for the valances and the table covering in the kitchen *right* provides the palette for the warm hues of the cabinets and floor. The curving tasseled edge of the cornice adds interest to the ordinary windows. Padded cornice boards strategically inject small quantities of special fabric. Create cornice boards by cutting plywood to specifications, wrapping boards with batting, and then stapling fabric onto the boards.

■ Curtains transform a whitewashed kitchen *above* from too cool to just right. A simple pleated floral valance hangs above matching cafe-style pinch-pleat panels. A complementary rose-printed fabric panel serves as a casual pantry door, keeping baskets and dry goods corralled.

■**DESIGN TIP** Use pastel floral-print fabrics to add romance to any room, especially living rooms, dining rooms, and bedrooms. When putting two florals together, always vary the print size, as shown in the kitchen *above*, and choose patterns that use the same color palette.

■ To bring a fresh look to your kitchen, change the valance and the accessories seasonally. Perky red accessories tie the kitchen decorating scheme together *right*. Checkered valances trimmed in yellow welting pay homage to the linens popular in the 1940s. Fruit-decked napkin rings hide the cup hooks that hold the valances in place. A tiny cherry ornament dangles from the bottom of each teardrop, adding a playful touch. The checkered fabric is repeated in the kitchen linens, jazzing up the tabletop.

■ Simple woven roller shades control sunlight in the kitchen *opposite*. The unassuming shades keep the focus on the woodland view—and on the kitchen's classic interior design. The shades can be rolled up and out of the way when cooking spatters are a possibility. The flax shades can also be wiped down with a damp cloth if they become soiled.

■ A wooden cornice board topped with crown molding doubles as a display shelf above the sink windows in the kitchen *above*. The fabric cloud shade mounted behind the cornice adds warm, vibrant color and softens the hard lines of the cabinetry and the tile. The shade can be lowered or raised easily with the tug of a cord.

bed&bath

Privacy and light control are the issues that typically need to be addressed in these private spaces.

FOR WINDOWS THAT FACE THE STREET OR A NEARBY NEIGHBOR, CHOOSE LINED PANELS, OPERATIVE SHUTTERS, OR LIGHT-CONTROLLING BLINDS, then add form to function by using attractive top treatments or side panels to enhance your room's decor.

Unify the various elements of the room with fabrics—choose a window treatment fabric that complements the bed linens, the upholstered furniture pieces, and the shower curtain. For variety, emphasize one fabric color in the bedroom and another in the adjoining bath.

■ In the cottage-style bedroom *right* operative shutters with wide louvers let in as much light as possible during the day and provide complete privacy during the evening. The simple window treatment allows the soft fabric of the fainting couch and the bed to stand out.

Cascading swags installed inside the window frames dress the top portion of the bedroom windows *top left* while cafe curtains offer a touch of privacy on the lower half of the windows. The floral chintz swag fabric links with the wallpaper border and highlights the mellow sage color scheme of the room. For a similar look that offers more privacy, hang the swags on or above the window frame and install lined, white pleated shades or undercurtains to cover the full window below each swag.

The triangular banner shapes in the valance *below left* give this master suite a tailored look. The bottom points of the triangles are finished with tassels that draw the eye up and out to the lakeside view beyond. Drapery panels installed behind the valance stack back to barely cover the trim on the sliding door, opening the room to the view during the day. The fully lined panels also provide privacy during the nighttime hours. The taupe color scheme creates a serene atmosphere that invites relaxation at the end of a hard day.

■ A lightweight polyester-nylon sheer fabric lets the sun shine into the bedroom *above.* Thick green piping and large, luxurious tassels finish the valance edge. Heavy string and sunburst shape tiebacks attach the window to the wall just above the window frame. The sheer panel is actually a part of the valance; only a fold separates the two. Each panel drapes the full length of the window and, for visual interest, sweeps to one side with the help of another tieback.

■ Use feminine floral patterns to make your window treatments serve as romantic backdrops. In the bedroom *right,* custom-made floor-to-ceiling overdraperies fabricated from the same material as the comforter are topped with beige silk necklace swags. The tone-on-tone swags provide visual relief from the large floral pattern. Pleated sheer underpanels protect the designer fabrics from the full sun.

■ Let clever hardware transform a treatment from plain to perfect. Simple crown swags attach to the arched window *above* with decorative iron tiebacks. Pulling the fabric through the flower-shape tiebacks creates the cinched pleats. A slightly modified treatment tops a rectangular window to the left of the bed, giving visual continuity to the room.

■ Grand arch-top windows in a 19th-century house inspired a sunny garden ambience in the bath *above left*. Stationary Roman shades, made from a lively botanical print fabric, mount below the window arches. The treatment permits an abundance of daylight while still offering adequate privacy. Covered buttons hold the soft pleats in place and enhance the contoured look of the shades.

■ Green-on-green striped Roman shades in a bath *above center* are hung just below the ceiling molding to make the windows appear taller than they actually are. Heavier upholstery-weight fabric creates more-tailored folds, which suit the trim styling of the room.

■ Tab-top sheer valances attach to decorative curtain rods mounted inside the windows of the bath *above right*. The valances conceal simple white blinds that can be pulled down and shut when privacy is necessary. The window adjacent to the door is fitted with glass shelves to show off a prized collection of vintage bottles.

■**DESIGN TIP** When moving into a new home that is void of window treatments, consider decorating your windows in stages. Start by adding privacy coverings, such as blinds or shutters, to the bedroom and bath windows. Add valances, side treatments, and window jewelry as time and budget allow. Adorn windows in public gathering spaces last.

draperies&
curtains

draperydesign

Whether your look is formal or casual, contemporary or traditional, use draperies or curtains to accentuate your decorating scheme.

UNPARALLELED IN THEIR VERSATILITY, THESE FABRIC-BASED TREATMENTS CAN ADD STYLE, CONTROL LIGHT, AND ENHANCE OR CONCEAL A VIEW. Although the terms are often used interchangeably, drapery panels are usually more formal in appearance than curtain panels.

Normally lined, pleated, and floor-length, drapery panels often attach by hooks to a traverse rod. A cord mechanism that hangs behind either the left or right panel draws both of the panels open and closed. Because of the way a traverse rod works, drapery panels don't always stack back as compactly as curtain panels do, so if a window has minimal wall space around it, you may want to consider curtains or another type of treatment. Before you purchase draperies, check their stackback, the technical term for the width of a window treatment when fully retracted.

Because draperies are typically pleated and more tailored in appearance, they generally lend a more traditional look to a decorating scheme than curtains do.

■ Fabric, color, and hardware choices give the traditional pinch-pleated design of the window dressings a contemporary flair. Sheer purple fabrics hung on silver rings and rods soften the business-suit look of the gray pinstriped wallpaper. A translucent voile in lavender creates a valance-like overlay.

Fabric selections, however, can dress up or dress down a drapery panel so that these convenient window coverings can be used in almost any decor.

■ Linen draperies that wrap the corner of this contemporary living room *left* unify arched multipaned windows and standard double-hung windows. The clean, uncluttered look fits the sleek decor of the apartment and brings an illusion of height to the room.

■ Choose window treatment fabrics that enhance the look of your upholstered furnishings. Deep gold tone and platinum-striped silk panels *above* blend beautifully with

■DESIGN TIP Because of the expense of fabrics in drapery and curtain panels, consider making your panels as versatile as possible so that they can move from home to home with you. Make gathers fuller than necessary and let panels puddle onto the floor; in your next home they can be shortened or used as is. Sew extra-wide hems and use swags that can be put together in sections; then you can fit them to windows of different widths.

the furnishings. Fringed edges add subtle texture. Pleated sheer panels mounted behind the draperies control sunlight. The faux-stone rod adds weight to the design.

■ Sheer linen panels atop matchstick blinds create an airy, see-through look in an eclectic living room *right*. The light-filtering blinds disguise a ho-hum view yet allow some sunlight to penetrate the room.

■ Black and white toile draperies *below* set off a collection of transferware plates and highlight the Palladian window. Thick white rods draw attention to the detailed woodwork around the window. The clever placement of the plates on the window trim makes the collection part of the room's focal point.

■ To make your windows seem taller, use crown molding as a top treatment. *Above,* crown molding doubles as a cornice, drawing attention to the 10-foot-high ceiling. The simple white pleated floor-to-ceiling draperies can be drawn to cover both the windows and patio doors.

curtaincharacter

Enliven your decor with any type of flowing fabric: panels, cafe curtains, or curtains shirred on both top and bottom rods.

CURTAINS ARE TYPICALLY LIGHTWEIGHT, UNLINED, AND SUSPENDED FROM A ROD BY SIMPLE TABS, RINGS, OR A ROD-POCKET CASING. Most can be drawn back by hand to create a simple, casual-looking window treatment. Lining the panels and adding decorative accessories and top treatments can make curtains look as elegant as any drapery panel.

Basic curtain panels are easy to make and install. They may cover the full length of the window or reach from ceiling to floor. Cafe curtains cover only the lower portion of the window, allowing light and views through the top half of the window. Panels shirred on rods at both the top and the bottom are somewhat stationary and are good solutions for swinging doors and for casement windows that swing in. For more information on combination treatments, see page 126.

■ The luxurious golden tieback panels create the illusion of much larger windows: The tiebacks stop where each window ends, but the floor-to-ceiling panels run the remaining lengths of the walls and meet at the corner. In keeping with the room's crisp traditional styling, the spacing between each of the looped fabric top tabs is carefully measured so that it is nearly identical.

■ The platinum-color linen and spun-rayon panels *below* hang from decorative brass L-hooks that attach to the wall a few inches above the transom window. Puddling the semi-sheer panels on the floor gives them an unstructured look against the room's linear architecture. Simple brass rings, hand-sewn along the top of the curtain panels, attach the panels to the hooks.

■ Plaid taffeta curtain panels soften the intense yellow of the dining room walls *above*. Lining and edging the gathered curtains with a complementary sage green print adds fullness and a touch of formality to the taffeta. The warm gold tone fabric complements the golden accessory pieces in the room, such as the old gold-leaf mirror and painted marble-topped side table.

■ Details do make the difference. Braided rope and unusual wooden tassels adorn the soft swags that top these simple white cotton-blend curtain panels *left*. Curved wrought-iron hardware draws the eye up and out to an attractive tree-lined yard.

■ Slender curtain panels *above* soften the expanse of wood and glass in this Arts and Crafts dining room. The berry-and-leaf motif that dresses up the cotton-linen panels was machine-embroidered and highlights the reproduction wallpaper frieze that enlivens the walls above the windows.

■ Cafe curtains *right* cover the lower half of a window, leaving a view through the top half. Like standard curtain panels, cafe curtains can be attached to a rod via tabs, ties, rings, or a rod pocket. These simple treatments suit casual decors and are easy to make and to hang.

■ Add impact with out-of-the-ordinary selections. Instead of solid wood or glass inset cabinet doors, plaid fabric, shirred on rods and hung inside the upper cabinet door frames, dresses up the kitchen *below*.

■**DESIGN TIP** Drafts and breezes can stir up curtain panels and rearrange the gathers in less-than-eye-pleasing ways. To minimize this unwanted movement, place curtain weights inside the hem pocket at each corner and at each vertical seam. The weights stabilize the panels and make them hang more symmetrically.

■ The sheer panel *above left* is made from less than a yard of fabric. Cut to fit the window exactly, the tailored panel does not gather at the top. A fabric loop attached to a simple chrome wall hook pulls the sheer back to one side. Substitute an opaque fabric for room-darkening qualities and privacy.

■ Curtains are an excellent choice in areas where there is little or no extra wall space. The red curtain panels *above center* have a small stackback, so that they can be drawn

back to within inches of the sidewalls. Throw pillows made from the same fabric as the curtain panels draw a touch of vibrancy into the modestly decorated family room.

■ Use nontraditional materials for one-of-a-kind window treatments. Navy blue tab-top curtains *above right* are attached to a decorative wooden rod with crisscrossed rope tied into slipknots. Hand-painted wooden leaves serve as the finials on the painted rod.

finishing touch: tabs

Whatever type of curtain or drapery you select, how you top it and tie it back can have a major impact on your design scheme.

■ Many tabs are sewn on, but the rounded tabs *above* are actually part of the curtain panel. To create the look, sew coordinating fabric pieces back-to-back, then fold the scalloped top of the panel over a rod and secure the tabs with buttons.

■ Rope tabs dock a nautical print fabric at the window *above right*. Fed through grommets and knotted, the ropes suspend the panel from boat cleats mounted to the wall.

■ Simple loops made from a coordinating fabric hold this curtain panel in place *opposite top left*. Square knots with draping tails sewn onto the bottom of the tabs put the ties into the spotlight.

■ When there's no call for a full-length panel, try a tab-top look that swags across the window *opposite top right*. Although it looks like one long piece, this treatment is really a series of double-sided oblong sections tied together over the rod with jute.

■ Old-fashioned covered buttons secure the checked tabs to the top of the floral panels *bottom right,* resembling the look of a little girl's overalls.

■ Matching fabric bows can be tied and then stitched to the top of curtain panels. Thicker, symmetrical bows *opposite bottom left* create a tailored appearance. Narrower, less-than-perfect bows *opposite bottom right* offer a more casual look.

finishing touch: ties

Instead of standard fabric ties, use found objects to add individual character to your drapery or curtain panels.

■ Curtain jewelry takes on new meaning with tiebacks fashioned from jeweled accessories. A necklace bauble adds pizzazz to the fabric tieback *above;* a vintage bracelet *above right* cinches a panel gathered at the center of a window.

■ A long black beaded necklace ties around a curtain for a quick and pretty hold *opposite top left.* A long gold chain or a strand of pearls can serve the same purpose. Dangle a locket or a special charm from the necklace for a romantic touch.

■ A rhinestone pin *opposite top right* sparkles in sunlight streaming through the window. A linen cocktail napkin wraps the curtain panel to hold it in place. The pin secures and decorates the napkin.

■ Sheer hair ribbons tied onto a simple metal bracelet adorn the breezy tieback panels *bottom right.* A similar look can be achieved using ribbons tied to copper wire.

■ A fabric rosette pinned to a tea towel holds back the panels *opposite bottom left.*

■ Prefer a more traditional approach? Most fabric stores carry tassels and rope in an array of colors. For a formal look, use matching silk ties like those *opposite bottom right* to adorn the tops and sides of your panels.

shades, shutters
&blinds

shades

Explore an array of styles to find a hardworking, good-looking shade that matches your needs.

SIMPLY DEFINED, A SHADE IS A WINDOW TREATMENT THAT CAN BE RAISED OR LOWERED BY A CORDING SYSTEM OR A SPRING. Style choices range from standard roll-up shades to more elaborate cascading fan shades, from tailored pleated shades to relaxed Roman shades to full balloon shades.

When raised, roller shades and pleated fabric shades virtually disappear, making them excellent choices for windows where you want to maximize the sunlight or showcase a gorgeous vista.

Roman shades add pattern, color, and a touch of softness without taking center stage. Billowing balloon shades and cascading fan shades convey romance.

Hard treatments—shutters, blinds, and pleated shades—take care of lighting and privacy concerns and work well alone or in combination with other treatment options.

■ For kitchen windows choose treatments that won't inhibit even the messiest chef. These designer fabric Roman shades fold up and out of the way when cooking is at a full boil. The buttery yellow and deep blue fabric complements the blue and bisque color scheme.

■ Golden silk fan shades *opposite* glow in the afternoon sunlight, bathing the living room in a warm buttercream haze. The single pleats accent the billowing cascade of silk and create deep, dramatic folds.

■ Creamy damask lines the floral fabric shade *above* to create a more uniform look from the outside. The stagecoach-style shades roll up to the desired position and are secured in place with ties. Because changing the position of the shade can be time-consuming, these shades work best on windows where frequent adjustments aren't necessary.

■ The inexpensive ready-made white canvas Roman shade *left* has been customized with an acrylic-paint pen. To ensure painting success, first mark the shade with pencil and then trace over your design with a paint pen.

■ Dress water-prone areas with waterproof treatments. The shades in the bath *below* are handwoven from a natural material called flax. Splashes from the tub don't hurt flax, and its natural look blends in beautifully with the limestone tub surround. Walls glazed with parchment-paper-look coverings complement the window treatments and set off the white woodwork.

■ Painting a plain white roller shade with acrylic paints makes this window *opposite top* resemble a garden trellis. The hand-drawn design complements the room's garden-theme decor. Properly installed, a spring-loaded roller shade is safe for a baby's room because it doesn't have a cord.

■ A pleated shade *opposite bottom* can be installed to fold up from the bottom or down from the top. Offering excellent privacy and light control, pleated shades fold back compactly (a 6-foot-long shade can pull back to under 3 inches); so this feature makes them a popular window covering choice. A honeycomb version of this shade, which features two layers of fabric that fold in opposite directions, is called a cellular shade and provides additional insulation and more protection from ultraviolet rays from the sun.

shutters

Use custom-made shutters to fit any window, including arches and eyebrows.

LOUVERED SHUTTERS ARE AVAILABLE IN THREE STYLES: CAFE SHUTTERS, PLANTATION SHUTTERS, AND SLIDING SHUTTERS. Like cafe curtains, cafe shutters cover only the bottom portion of a window. Plantation shutters cover a window from top to bottom. Plantation shutters can also be made from solid wood panels for complete privacy and light blockage, or they can be fitted with fabric panels that have been inserted into a wooden frame. Some hinge in the middle and fold back within the window frame, while others open completely like a cabinet door. Sliding shutters work like sliding patio doors and operate on a track where one door slides behind the other.

■ White wooden shutters control the glare from west-facing windows without inhibiting the view of the garden. Hinged on one side, shutters can be fully opened but are often left closed with only the louvers open. To match the light throughout the day, slat angles can be changed by simply pulling up or down on the center vertical strip.

■ Much like cabinet doors, the shutters in the living room *opposite* do not fold because they are hinged on only one side. Painted an aged white to match the color of the adobe walls, the simple wooden shutters blend with the Southwestern design scheme and keep the primary focus on the fireplace and furnishings.

■ Paint shutters to highlight furnishings. Green-painted plantation shutters frame this attic office window *above*. The same hue appears in some of the upholstered furnishings and complements the earth tones of the carpeting.

■ Folding solid-wood cafe shutters *left* provide enough privacy for a bath. A simple white cloud shade adorns the top half of the window and controls sunlight.

blinds

Versatile and affordable, blinds fit a variety of decors and are an excellent starting point on windows where privacy or light control is a concern.

LIKE SHUTTERS, BLINDS COME IN THREE VARIETIES: Woven blinds are similar in construction to roller shades; venetian blinds have horizontal movable slats similar to those found in plantation shutters; and vertical blinds have slats that run up and down instead of side to side.

Woven blinds are typically made from thin strips of natural fibers, usually cane or basswood, that have been woven together with twine or thread. Woven blinds can also be made from vinyl slats. Called quills, the thin horizontal strips in woven blinds filter daylight but do not offer complete privacy. Venetian blinds are typically made from wood, aluminum, or vinyl and are an excellent choice for both light control and privacy. Vertical blinds are often made from vinyl or stiffened fabric. Like their horizontal counterparts, vertical blinds offer excellent privacy and light control.

Crisp blinds dress the windows in this contemporary apartment. A mirror on the adjacent wall reflects the natural light and creates the illusion of more windows.

■ Customize blinds with optional fabric tapes. Sunny yellow decorative fabric tapes add a touch of color to these aluminum venetian blinds *below.* The blinds complement the clean lines of the Arts and Crafts decor.

■ The blinds *opposite* are made from fabric louvers softened by a sheer-fabric encasement. A battery-powered remote control makes it possible to open and close all the blinds, even those out of reach, with only the push of a button.

■ A sheer fabric encases the vertical blinds *above left,* softening hard lines and offering more light control. An unusual white wooden cornice tops the blinds and draws attention up and out to the view beyond.

■ Split-bamboo blinds filter afternoon sun in a dining area *above center*. The natural

blinds complement the painted cane chairs and fit the gardenlike setting.

Decorative brown fabric tapes added to standard wooden blinds set off the two-tone cabinets and rustic table in this tiny kitchen *above right*. On cloudy days, the blinds can be pulled up to a stack of 3 inches to let in as much light as possible.

toptreatments

toptreatments

Make a dramatic style statement with affordable valances, swags and jabots, upholstered or wooden cornices, or interior awnings.

RELATIVELY SMALL IN SIZE, TOP TREATMENTS PACK A BIG DECORATIVE PUNCH. Use them alone or combine them with shades or blinds for privacy and light control. Pair them with operative or fixed draperies for a more luxurious look.

VALANCES. Originally designed to conceal window treatment hardware, valances are now used to tie together windows and doors of different shapes and sizes and to enhance the decor of a room. Because valances typically hang down less than a foot, choose fabric with a print small enough to fit within the valance dimensions, but not so small that the design becomes unrecognizable when viewed from a short distance.

Fabric selection determines whether your valance is more formal or more casual in appearance. Lightweight, sheer fabrics tend to flutter with the breeze; weighty fabrics tend to add more substance to your window. Choose the look that best fits your decor.

■ A custom-designed leaded and beveled glass window sheds light on the food preparation area of this kitchen. The shirred blue and white Spode-print fabric valance underscores the beauty of the window and complements a collection of Spode china. The same fabric pops up on the barstool cushions and on the gathered valance in the adjacent dining room.

■ To make a kitchen look warm and welcoming without overwhelming the room, use a simple valance that blends with the wall color. Old-fashioned white buttons set off the draped and pleated valance *above*. The focal point of the work area is the glass-front cabinets, not the window, so a cream color fabric was selected to blend in with the walls.

■ A little more than a yard of leaf-print fabric brings a ho-hum kitchen cleanup center to life *opposite top*. Gathering tape lifts the fabric into simple pleats; two rows

of hand-sewn satin trim draw the eye up to the fabric and out toward the view.

■ Views of an orchard served as the inspiration for the breakfast room decor *opposite bottom*. Pleated fruit-print fabric valances add cheerful color. The checkerboard motif of the painted walls reappears in smaller form in the lining of the valances and on the top ties of the matching cafe curtains.

■ Add texture and interest with colorful trim. In this rendition of the popular balloon shade *above*, an ornate fringe header adds life to the two-fabric valance. The valance combines a lightweight cotton floral with a heavier striped canvas lining to give the treatment body and to create deeper folds.

■ No, it isn't a roller shade; it just looks like one. Made from an expensive brocade, this gently curved valance *opposite top* adds color to a home office without breaking the budget. A sturdy wooden rod and tassels set off the top and bottom edge, respectively.

■ Stretch your budget by mixing pricey fabrics with more affordable ones. Less than a yard of paisley-print designer fabric was needed to make this two-tone valance *opposite bottom*.

■DESIGN TIP A little fabric goes a long way in a decorative valance. If your budget is tight, use the most expensive fabrics for your valances. Use any leftover scraps to cover or trim pillows or to cover chair cushions. Use less expensive materials for underpanels or install ready-made blinds underneath custom-made top treatments to control light or provide privacy.

SWAGS AND JABOTS. Classic styling makes swags and jabots the most enduring top treatment. Ideal in many settings, swags and jabots look particularly stunning in formal rooms with tall ceilings and elaborate furnishings. Swags can be either flat and smooth or full of pleats; jabots can drape to mid-window or stop a foot or two down.

■ Semi-sheer swags *opposite* combine with matching tieback panels to create a light and breezy look in this casually elegant living room. Choosing a more opaque fabric would make the room appear darker.

■ For drama and ease of opening the patio doors, a flowing swag *above* is mounted high above the door frame on a rod measuring nearly 2 feet wider than the doors. A solid taupe lining gives the swag more body and creates a uniform look from outside.

■ Three different prints, all in the same weight of chintz, make up these one-of-a-kind swags *above*. Subdued pinstriped blue jabots and soft chiffon yellow walls prevent the colorful high-country mix from overwhelming the room. The table runner repeats one of the patterns from the swags, as do the toss pillows on the window seat. Although each fabric has a decidedly different pattern, a shared color palette ensures compatibility. Lining gives the treatment a uniform look from outside, and interlining prevents the patterns from showing through.

■ Crisp linen swags and matching flowing curtains add a traditional touch to the bedroom *opposite top*. Use neutral-tone window treatments and wallcoverings to create a soothing space that is ideal for relaxing before and after a busy day.

■ White terry cloth swags add a charming touch to this sophisticated master bath *opposite bottom*. Because the terry is thick and heavy, the swags drape beautifully.

■DESIGN TIP Different hanging techniques convey different degrees of formality. A loosely hung gathered swag imparts a casual look. A crisply pleated, precisely hung swag and jabot treatment suggests more formality.

CORNICES. Although cornices are more tailored in appearance than valances, they perform the same decorative function. If sun control or privacy is a concern, pair cornices with blinds or shades. Upholstered cornices provide a softer look than their wooden counterparts.

■ Upholstered cornice boards are inexpensive and easy to make. The secret to the homemade cornice lies in a board that's mounted to the wall with two L-brackets. The window topper *below* was created by stapling a sheet of foam

padding over a piece of lightweight plywood. Colorful striped fabric was then stapled to the top of the board. The rest of the fabric hangs loose. For added flair, lined navy triangles cut to the width of each window were hand-sewn on top of the striped fabric. Bright yellow buttons add a final flourish.

▪ Use window treatments to draw attention to the best architectural feature in a room. Green-painted crown molding *above* flows from the family room's built-in storage to the adjacent windows. The natural pine cornice below the molding matches the wood used for the built-in, creating a tailored look.

■ The cornice board in this all-white kitchen *below* doubles as a display shelf for collectibles. A simple valance softens the lower edge of the shelf, easing the transition between the hard treatment and the soft lace cafe panels that cover the lower half of the window.

■ The wide wooden cornice that tops this bedroom windows *opposite top* is painted to match the walls. The burgundy-trimmed rectangles resemble architectural embellishment, adding design punch for little cost.

■ Painted to look like colorful swags and jabots, this wooden window treatment *left* is ideal for kitchen use. A quick wipe with a wood cleaner removes grease buildup and kitchen spatters. To create a similar look in your kitchen, use a jigsaw to cut a cornice board from thin plywood. Use stencils to mimic a floral fabric design.

■**DESIGN TIP** If sun control and privacy are a concern, pair cornices or valances with miniblinds or fabric shades. To avoid starkness, opt for blinds or shades in a color that blends with the walls.

AWNINGS. Interior awnings can add a new dimension and a touch of sun control to your windows. Awnings visually connect windows of different sizes and styles (like valances do), and they can also break up a boxy room, offering extra depth and angular interest. Interior awnings can be made from a variety of fabrics, including sturdy canvas as well as other heavy cottons and cotton blends.

■ The awning-like window treatment in the child's room *above left* is actually a fabric-covered cornice board. Red fabric triangles and yellow painted wooden balls create a night-

cap-shape trim. The colorful carousel-horse fabric is repeated in the crib bedding.

■ Fresh flowers, patio chairs, and a custom-made interior awning make dining inside this kitchen *above center* feel like dining alfresco. To give the treatment more visual weight and to create a consistent color scheme from the outside, have two treatments made and mount one slightly above the other.

■ The heavyweight cotton awning treatment *above right* adds cheerful color to this country kitchen. The windows end at the cabinet tops, but the awning makes the windows appear to extend to the ceiling.

combinations

combinations

Give your windows a polished look by putting winning combinations of window dressings to work in your home.

OUTFITTING YOUR WINDOWS HAS NEVER BEEN EASIER. Whether you choose treatments that are custom- or ready-made, or some of each, you can combine practical options, such as shades and blinds, with attractive top treatments or side panels to create a personal look.

Let your imagination guide you. Envision how you want your rooms to look and then work toward turning your dreams into reality.

Although your windows may not look exactly like those featured here, most treatment styles and color palettes are easily transferable. Your ultimate goal is to produce window treatments that meet all your functional goals while adding beauty and style to your rooms.

■ Practical roller shades, purposely chosen in a color to blend with the parlor walls, hang behind stately full-length draperies. Together the treatments disguise where the wall ends and where the windows begin. These eye-fooling treatments make the windows and doors appear to be the same height. Mounting the shade high above the glass door also prevents interference with the door swing.

■ In a traditionally dressed living room *below,* a creamy swag blends with the walls, keeping the primary focus on the central mantel area and artwork. Fringed edges add the right amount of formality to meld the window treatment with the decor. Tucked behind the swag, pleated shades control sunlight.

■ Loose folds of flowing fabric bring additional old-world flavor into the ornate room *opposite.* When architecture and decor are of a grand scale, use layers of heavily gathered or pleated fabric to give windows proper presence in the room.

■ Billowing pleats and gathers soften hard lines in this dreamy bedroom window reading nook *left*. The valance offsets sheer flowing cloud shades; together they add fairy-tale charm to the romantically embellished room. Gathered side panels tuck behind cozy cushions that beckon young and old to nestle in for a good read.

■ Tailored panels and a loosely gathered valance are the perfect treatment choice for Craftsman-era windows *above*. The five-square design on the valance and side panels is made up of appliqued coordinating fabric swatches. This design and the wallpaper both reflect the understated elegance of the Craftsman era. The velvet tieback panel in the foreground serves as a divider between the dining area and the living room, recalling a common decorating touch from the early 20th century.

■ To completely cover a bay window with one pair of draperies instead of a pair for each separate window, hang panels in front of the bay, as shown *right*. Roman valances soften the windowpanes when the panels are tied back.

■ A casually gathered valance softens the edges of the casement window *below*. Because the window opens in, the valance is installed on a hinged rod that gracefully shifts to the side; the tieback sheer hangs from a rod attached to the window frame itself.

■DESIGN TIP Where you install tiebacks affects the perceived shape of your windows. When curtain or drapery panels are tied back high, windows appear taller and narrower. When panels are tied back low, as shown *above,* windows seem wider than their actual dimensions.

■ The diamond-pattern upholstered cornice board *above left* adds height and prominence to the breakfast room window, transforming it into a focal point of the sleekly furnished room. Instead of the usual side panels, sheer curtains below the valance hang one in front of the other on double rods. The outermost panel ties in the center, creating a symmetrical look that sets off the contemporary styling.

■ Gold and silver unite on the tailored panels *above center*. The

panels stack back several inches beyond the window frame, making the narrow window seem wider. A pleated shade mounted inside the window frame controls light.

■ When combining checked and floral patterns, choose fabrics that have hues of similar intensities and that share some colors as shown *above right*. The old-fashioned balloon shade and side panel combination complements the dining room's high-country style.

■DESIGN TIP Combination treatments give you freedom to manipulate the perceived size and shape of your windows. An inside-mount shade, for example, emphasizes the actual size of a window; mounted outside the frame, the same treatment makes the window appear larger. Hanging a valance above a window so that the bottom edge barely covers the top of the window glass, as shown *opposite left,* makes a window appear taller. To shorten a tall window, hang the valance so that the top edge lies slightly above the window frame.

■ Loosely gathered Kingston pleats flow into cascading swags on the bedroom valance *below*. The toile print of the valance and drapery side panels complements the vintage design of the room. A sheer checkered balloon shade diffuses daylight and protects bed linens and antique furnishings from sun damage.

■ Nineteenth-century reproduction fabrics adorn the Kingston-pleated bed crown and the matching window valance *opposite*. The crown, combined with tightly gathered layers of undersheers, gives prominence to the upholstered bed and puts the well-dressed side window in its proper place.

■DESIGN TIP Choose a pattern that corresponds to the scale of your room. Small-scale patterns are often used in small spaces where you can clearly see the design from anywhere in the room. A large room can support an ample-size pattern. Oversize, busy patterns visually contract space, creating the impression that a room is smaller than it actually is.

■ Plaid panels tied back high on the wall make the corner windows in the bedroom *opposite top* look tall and stately. Generously proportioned decorative rods give the window tops additional prominence. Undersheers lend a touch of privacy. The illusion of extra height helps the windows match the scale of the elevated sleighbed and lofty fireplace mantel.

■ Gathered valances edged in blue ruffles unite window treatment and bed dressing in the bedroom *opposite*

bottom. The timeless blue and white color scheme adds a classic touch to the cottage decor and is an excellent choice for a rarely redecorated guest bedroom. Traverse rods make opening and closing the drapery panels a breeze.

■ The window fabric selections in the bedroom *above* are inspired by the cheerful plate collection that surrounds the exterior door. Bright floral chintz valances and side panels draw attention to the corner windows and the tree-lined yard beyond.

■ Super-versatile tab-top sheer panels soften the look of light-filtering blinds on the window *above*. The neutral fabric and blinds blend into the background, allowing the colorful bed linens to be the center of attention.

■ Roman shades and rod-pocket panels made from a colorfully dotted fabric bring a sense of playfulness to a child's bedroom windows *right*. Louvered shutters, instead of corded blinds, enable the child to safely control the amount of light that enters the room without aid from an adult.

help&how-to

help&how-to

Planning and preparation are the keys to successfully executed window treatments.

FOR INFORMATION ON FABRIC SELECTIONS, SEE THE *FIBER & FABRIC PRIMER* ON PAGES 148-151. To find specific solutions for a variety of window and door types, review the *Window & Door Sketchbook* beginning on page 152. If you hire a professional to design your window treatments, he or she will most likely measure the windows and have the treatments professionally installed. If you plan to purchase ready-made or made-to-order window treatments, or if you plan to make your own window treatments, see the *Window Measuring Guide* on page 158.

■ The best window treatments can be thought of as a series of small but important choices. Select the best fabric, a pleasing style, and appropriate trim— then install the treatments in a professional manner.

fiber&fabric primer

Fabric affects the appearance of your treatment more than any other factor does. Quality materials drape well and have more body than fabrics with lower thread counts, creating a fuller, richer appearance.

NATURAL FIBERS.

■ **Cotton.** Durable, strong, and affordable, cotton as shown *opposite top right* dyes easily and blends well with other fabrics. Weight affects how cotton fabric drapes; higher thread counts wear better. Machine-washable, the fabric wrinkles and mildews in damp environments unless treated and may eventually yellow or fade in the sun.

■ **Linen.** Durable and very strong, linen, as shown in the sheer panel *opposite bottom left,* has nice texture and is somewhat resistant to sun and mildew. More expensive than cotton, linen tends to be stiff when draping, and it wrinkles easily. Most linen is dry clean only.

■ **Silk.** This costly, lustrous, strong fabric *opposite top left* drapes beautifully and resists mildew. Colors have a jewel-like tone. Unless treated, water will spot silk and bright colors may fade in the sun. Designer silks require dry cleaning.

■ **Wool.** Durable and strong, wool *opposite bottom right* dyes well and drapes easily. Moderately priced, this dry-clean-only fabric is an excellent insulator. Unless chemically treated, wool attracts moths and weakens over time when in direct sunlight.

SYNTHETIC FIBERS.

■ **Acrylic.** Wool-like in texture, this fabric resists both mildew and moths. Moderately priced and typically hand-washable, it is not as durable as wool and has a tendency to pill.

■ **Acetate.** Although not as strong as natural fibers, this synthetic material has a silklike appearance and drapes well. Wrinkle-resistant and affordable, acetate is typically dry clean only.

■ **Nylon.** Strong, durable, and hand-washable, affordable nylon fabrics *above* are wrinkle-free. Higher thread count improves draping.

■ **Polyester.** Durable and strong, polyester resists wrinkles and moths and drapes well. Textures vary from slick to nubby. The fabric gradually loses strength from exposure to the sun. Moderately priced, polyester can usually be machine washed and dried.

■ **Rayon.** Weaker than the other fibers listed, rayon drapes well and offers good coloration. Its texture can be made to resemble silk or linen. Affordably priced, rayon does wrinkle and typically requires dry cleaning.

■**DESIGN TIP** Purchase decorator fabrics, not garment fabrics. Although more costly, decorator fabrics have higher thread counts and tighter weaves for longer wear. Because decorator fabrics are sold in 54-inch widths, you need less yardage than with standard 45-inch-wide garment fabrics. To ensure a perfect color match, order all your fabric at one time.

FABRICS.

Your fabric selection determines how much color, pattern, and texture your window treatment will have. Fabric prices vary depending on the type and quality of material from which they are made.

■ **Brocade.** A weighty formal fabric woven of cotton, wool, or silk, brocade features a raised floral design that resembles embroidery.

■ **Canvas.** Available in a range of weights, this coarsely woven cotton material is strong and inexpensive.

■ **Chintz.** This cotton weave is coated with a high-luster glaze and often features a floral motif.

■ **Damask.** Made from a Jacquard weave of cotton, silk, or wool, damask *opposite bottom right* is known for its textural contrast of two finishes, matte and satin.

■ **Gingham.** This crisp cotton fabric *below* is woven into block or checked prints.

■ **Lace.** Made from cotton or a cotton-polyester blend, this popular fabric *right* features an openwork, crochet-like, or eyelet design.

■ **Moiré.** Made from silk or a synthetic, this fabric is coated with a finish that resembles watermarking.

■ **Organdy.** An acid wash produces the crisp finish of this lightweight cotton.

■ **Satin.** Made from silk, linen, or a cotton weave, satin features a glossy finish on the right side and a dull finish on the back.

■ **Sheers.** Soft, translucent fabrics such as voile or lace, these textiles vary in opacity and gently diffuse light.

■ **Taffeta.** This crisp, almost stiff, shiny silk or acetate weave retains its shape with little support.

■ **Tapestry.** This heavy woven cloth, used for panel trim *opposite top right,* is made from a variety of natural fibers and features a pictorial design.

■ **Toile.** This tightly woven cotton features a pastoral scene printed in one color *opposite top left.*

■ **Velvet.** Woven of silk, cotton, linen, rayon, or wool, velvet has a furlike texture *opposite bottom left* that blocks drafts and light.

■ **Voile.** Also known as muslin, voile is woven from cotton and has a texture that ranges from coarse to fine.

■**DESIGN TIP** To test a fabric's draping ability, gather at least 2 yards of the material in your hand and let the other end drop. If the fabric naturally falls into attractive folds, it is a good candidate for a swag or panel. This procedure also lets you see how the fabric pattern looks when pleated or gathered.

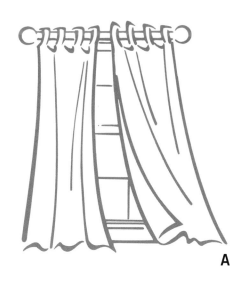

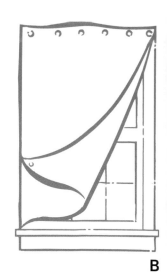

A

B

window&doorsketchbook

Don't know which treatment works for your window? Find the illustration that best matches your window design and check out your options.

SINGLE WINDOWS. If you're dressing a single window, consider whether you want it to be more or less noticeable. Add fullness with flowing curtains or tiebacks, as shown in figures A, D, and E. If its scale matches the other elements in your room, give the window a top treatment as shown in figure C or a simple panel as shown in figure B. If you don't want to draw attention to a window, treat it with a plain shade or blind in a color that matches your walls or woodwork.

MULTIPLE/MATCHED SERIES. A series of identical windows invites sunlight into your home. These windows offer a variety of decorating options. To keep the focus on the view and the architectural artistry of your windows, use a top treatment only, as shown in figure F. If you need a dressing that offers more privacy or light control, mount shades or blinds inside each window molding, as shown in figures G and H. Individual interior mountings offer a tailored look. If you prefer a fuller treatment, options range from to-the-floor draperies, as shown in figure I, to draperies topped with cornices or valances, as shown in figures J and K.

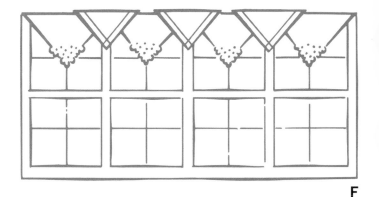

F

I

C

D

E

G

H

J

K

CORNER WINDOWS. As shown in figures L through P, mirror-image window dressings allow you to treat corner windows separately but achieve the effect of a single design. Use draperies or vertical blinds that draw to the outside; check that blinds raise and lower without clashing. In small spaces, avoid fabrics with busy patterns and contrasting colors; instead, match treatments to wall color to blend them into the background and expand the room.

BAY AND BOW WINDOWS. Like corner windows, the windows within a bay or a bow may demand separate but equal treatments, as illustrated in figures Q through U. To keep things trim and tailored, use shades, blinds, or shutters, as shown in figures Q and R. To draw more attention to your treatment, add a swag or valance, as shown in figures S and T. For a formal look, install framing draperies across the front of the window alcove, as shown in figure U. For a curving bow window, use a flexible rod that can follow the curve in one sweep.

SLIDING DOORS. Sliding doors present a special decorating challenge. The covering must provide adequate privacy and light control, yet still allow the doors to operate freely. Blinds, fabric shades, draperies, and sliding panels are all options to consider. Illustrated in figures V through Z, mount them at the ceiling line and check that they draw totally to the side, so the walkway will be clear. To control light throughout the day, try a layered treatment of draperies over blinds.

HIGH WINDOWS. The goal in treating high windows is to visually enlarge them with long treatments or to make their design look purposeful. If you place a piece of furniture under the window, an exact-fit covering as shown in figures 1, 2, and 3 will stay out of the way. If your room is full of horizontal elements, such as beds and dressers, add visual interest with vertical, to-the-floor treatments, as shown in figures 4 and 5. To make windows appear larger, install a row of fixed shutters below the windows and operative shutters on the actual panes as shown in figure 2.

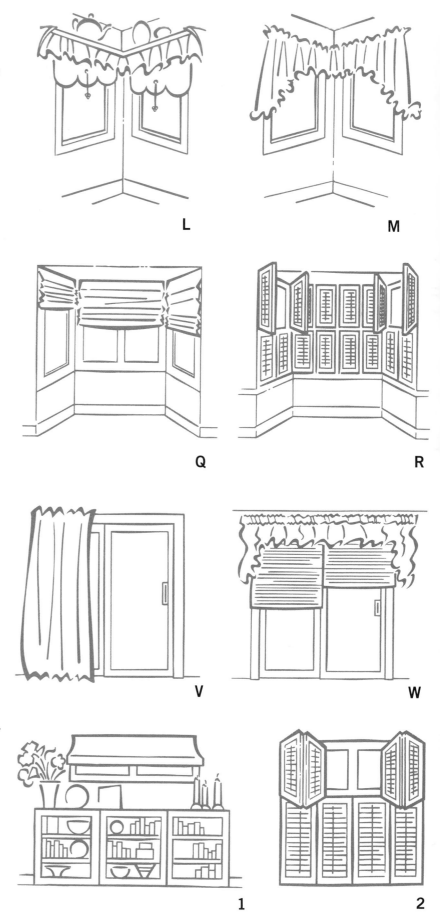

L

M

Q

R

V

W

1

2

N

O

P

S

T

U

X

Y

Z

3

4

5

CASEMENT WINDOWS. Standard casement windows open in or out and can be treated like single windows, as shown in figures 6 through 10. Newer windows offer fold-down cranks that do not interfere with window treatments. If you have a window model with a full-handle crank, mount a covering to the outside so that it clears the cranking mechanism. Swinging rods as shown in figure 6 or fixed curtain rods as shown in figure 7 also offer solutions. If you choose tiebacks, dress each window in a drapery panel that draws to the outer edge of the window where tieback hardware is installed. For inward-swinging casement windows, choose a treatment that doesn't interfere with window operation. Install curtains or blinds far enough above the window molding so that the treatment can be raised high enough to allow the windows to open freely.

FRENCH DOORS. French doors, as shown in figures 11 through 15, combine the decorating challenges of inward swinging casement windows with those of sliding glass doors. There are two basic solutions for these doors: Either affix your treatment to each individual door panel, or opt for a treatment that clears the doors by drawing completely to the side or top. For a look that won't conceal the architecture, mount blinds or shades on each door. If your decorating style calls for a softer touch, consider shirred lace panels or door-mounted tiebacks. If you prefer traditional drapery treatments, use a rod that extends well beyond the door frame so draperies can be drawn out of the way of the doors. If your French doors are topped with transoms, leave the upper windows bare, or treat the doors and windows as one, with the rod installed at the ceiling line.

SHAPELY WINDOWS. The trick to treating windows that have sculptural curves and unusual shapes is to flow with the shape of the opening. Where privacy and light control are needed, use custom-fitted shades, blinds, or shirred fabric. Palladian-inspired half-round windows are most spectacular when minimally dressed. For example, in a bedroom, add a privacy treatment to the lower part and leave the half-round bare for maximum natural light.

6

7

11

12

16

17

8

9

10

13

14

15

18

19

20

window measuring guide

Before purchasing ready-made or made-to-order treatments, learn how to measure your windows accurately.

To ensure accuracy, use a quality steel measuring tape. Decide whether you want your treatments to fit inside your window (an inside mount) or to cover your window (an outside mount), and then measure accordingly:

■ **Inside Mount.** For an inside mount, measure the opening width at the top, middle, and bottom of the window, recording the narrowest measurement. Do the same for the length, recording the longest measurement. Round your measurements to the closest ⅛ inch.

■ **Outside Mount.** For an outside mount, measure the opening width and add at least 3 inches to each side of the window opening if the wall space allows. Measure the opening length and add at least 2 inches in height for hardware and any overlap.

■ **Drapery Measurements.** To measure the drop for draperies, measure your windows from where you intend to install the rod to where you want the draperies to fall. For width, measure the full length of the rod. To calculate the length of a decorative scarf or a single fabric piece, measure the distance from the bottom of the drapery ring or the top of the rod to the point where you want the fabric to drape. Multiply that measurement by 2; add 10 inches to each side if you want the fabric to puddle on the floor. Measure the width of the area to be covered and add that figure to the length for the total yardage.

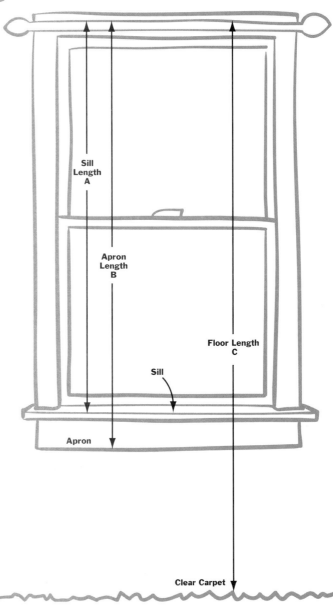

Sill Length A

Apron Length B

Floor Length C

Sill

Apron

Clear Carpet

A

Architectural style, 6, 14–19
Awnings, 124–125

B

Baby's room, 17, 96, 97
Balloon shades, 9, 13, 92, 114, 137, 138
Bathroom
    blinds, 32, 33
    shades, 68, 96
    shutters, 101
    swags, 32, 33, 118, 119
Bay windows, 10–11, 56, 57, 134–135, 154–155
Bedroom
    blinds, 33, 48–49, 142
    combination treatments for, 138–143
    cornice, 122, 123
    cottage-style, 48–49, 64
    curtains, 84
    draperies, 72–73
    shutters, 64, 142, 143
    swags, 65, 67, 118, 119
    valances, 65, 66, 138–139, 140, 141
Blinds
    for bathroom, 32, 33
    for bedroom, 33, 48–49, 142
    for light control, 13, 102
    matchstick, 44–45, 75
    mini-, 13, 44–45
    venetian, 102, 104
    vertical, 102, 106
Breakfast room, 11, 31, 112, 113, 136

C

Cafe curtains, 61, 64-65, 78, 83, 113, 122
Casement windows, 12, 59, 134, 156–157
Cellular shades, 13, 96, 97
Child's room, 13, 124, 142–143
Combination treatments, 126–143
Corner windows, 154–155
Cornices, 13, 19, 60, 61, 106, 120–123, 136
Crown molding, 13, 25, 58, 77, 121
Curtains
    cafe, 61, 64-65, 78, 83, 113, 122
    for dining room, 81, 82
    draperies versus, 72
    for family room, 85
    for kitchen, 61, 83
    tabs, 86–87
    ties, 88–89

D

Dining room
    blinds, 106–107
    casual, 30
    combination treatment for, 137
    curtains, 81, 82
    drapery, 56–57
    formal look for, 36, 37
    swags and jabots, 56, 118, 119
    valances, 30, 42, 43
Doors
    French, 6, 12, 23, 33, 54, 55, 59, 156–157
    patio, 117
    sliding, 154–155
Drapery
    for bedroom, 72–73, 138

in combination treatments, 128–129, 134, 135, 138
    and crown molding, 77
    curtains versus, 72
    for dining room, 42, 43, 56–57
    fabric selection for, 74–75
    and French doors, 12
    for living room, 52-53, 54, 74–75
    measurements, 158
    tabs, 86–87
    ties, 88–89

F

Fabric
    fiber and fabric primer, 148–151
    sunlight and, 6, 13
    thermally insulated, 13
    as uniting feature, 7, 64
Family room, 22, 40–41, 52, 53, 85, 121
French doors
    options for, 33, 54, 55, 156–157
    practical considerations for, 6, 12, 59

K

Kitchen
    awnings, 125
    blinds, 107
    cornices, 60-61, 63, 122, 123
    curtains, 61, 83
    shades, 38–39, 43, 62, 63, 92–93
    valances, 30, 31, 47, 62, 110–113

L-O

Light control, 6, 13, 92, 102
Living room
    combination treatments for, 128–131, 133
    draperies, 52-53, 54, 55, 74–75
    fan shades, 94, 95
    formal look for, 23, 34–35, 52
    shutters, 34–35, 98–100, 101
    swags, 116, 117, 130

Matchstick blinds, 44-45, 75
Measuring guide, 158
Miniblinds, 13, 44–45

Office, home, 25, 101, 114, 115

P-R

Plantation shutters, 32, 34–35, 44, 98, 101

Rods
    custom-made, 19
    hinged, 8–9, 134
    swing-arm, 13, 156
    traverse, 72, 140-141
Roman shades
    for bathroom, 68
    for bedroom, 48–49, 142–143
    for breakfast room, 57
    for family room, 22
    for kitchen, 38–39, 92–93

S

Shades. *See also* Roman shades
    for baby's room, 96, 97
    balloon, 9, 13, 92, 114, 137, 138
    for bathroom, 96
    for bedroom, 48–49, 142–143

cellular, 13, 96
    for kitchen, 38–39, 43, 92–93
    for light control, 13, 92
    for living room, 94, 95
    painted, 95, 96, 97
    roller, 46, 47, 62, 63, 92, 96, 97
Shutters
    for bedroom, 64, 142, 143
    for cottage charm, 11, 44
    for light control, 13
    plantation, 32, 34–35, 44, 98, 101
    for study, 38
    for sunroom, 32
Silk
    as formal fabric, 22, 23, 148
    for living room, 34–35, 94, 95
Sunlight, 6, 13, 92, 102
Swags
    for bathroom, 32, 33, 118, 119
    for bedroom, 64-65, 67, 118, 119
    for casual look, 28–29, 119
    for dining room, 56, 118
    for formal look, 20–21, 116, 119
    for home office, 25
    for living room, 116, 117, 130
    for sunroom, 10–11

T

Tabs, 86–87
Tassels, 14, 15, 19, 25, 56, 60, 61, 65, 66, 81, 88, 89
Ties, 88–89
Top treatments. *See also* Swags; Valances
    awnings, 124–125
    cornices, 13, 19, 60, 61, 106, 120–123, 136
    swags and jabots, 116–119
    valances, 110–115

V

Valances
    for bathroom, 69
    for bedroom, 65, 66, 138–139, 140, 141
    and French doors, 23
    for home office, 114, 115
    for kitchen, 30, 31, 47, 110–113
    and wallpaper, 57
Venetian blinds, 102, 104
Vertical blinds, 102, 106

W

Waterproof shades, 96
Window measuring guide, 158

U.S. UNITS TO METRIC EQUIVALENTS

To Convert From	Multiply By	To Get
Inches	25.4	Millimeters (mm)
Inches	2.54	Centimeters (cm)
Feet	30.48	Centimeters (cm)
Feet	0.3048	Meters (m)

METRIC UNITS TO U.S. EQUIVALENTS

To Convert From	Multiply By	To Get
Millimeters	0.0394	Inches
Centimeters	0.3937	Inches
Centimeters	0.0328	Feet
Meters	3.2808	Feet